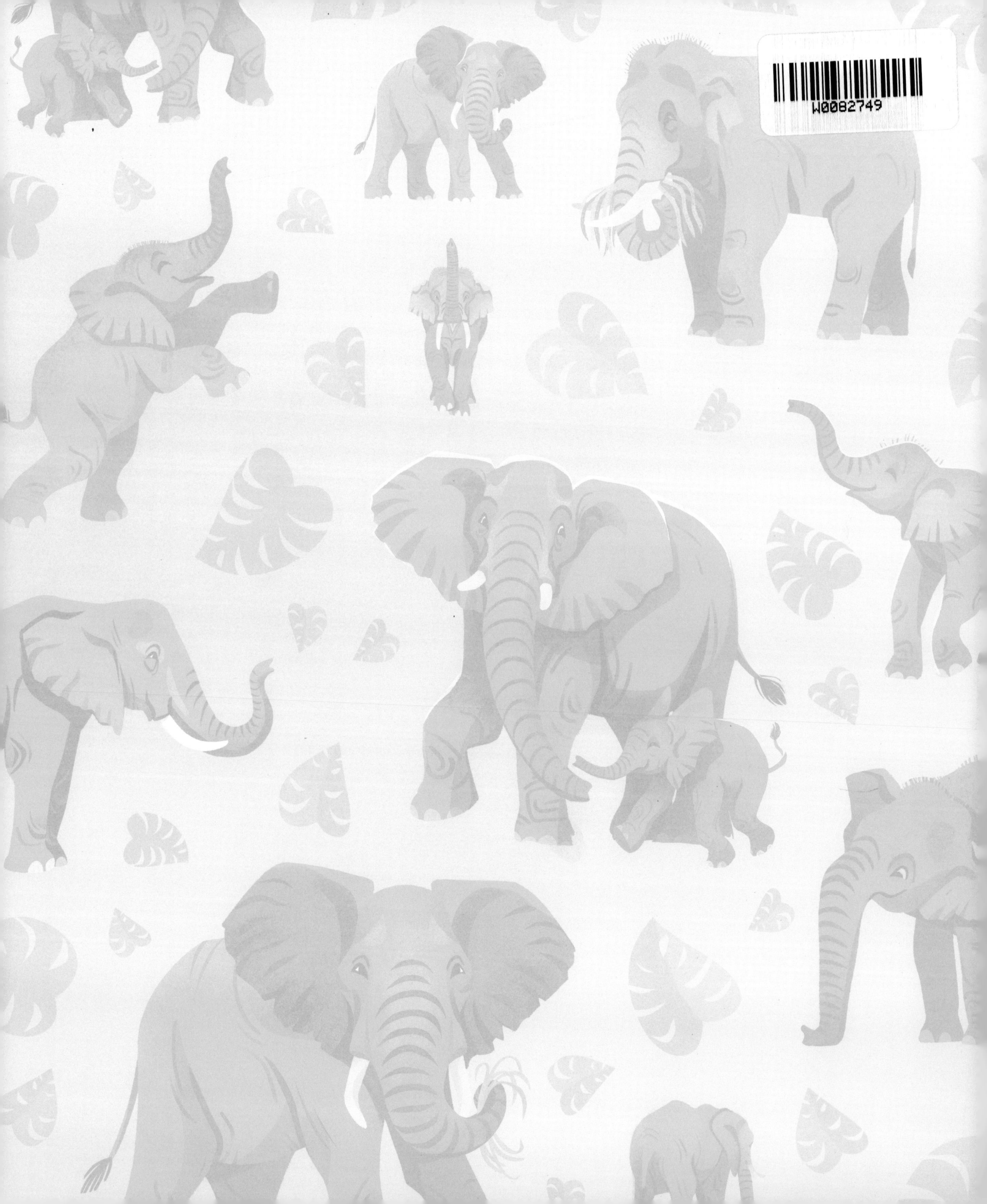

OTHER BOOKS BY EMMA FLANNERY AND TIM FLANNERY

Sensational Sharks

Explore Your World: Weird, Wild, Amazing!

Explore Your World: Deep Dive into Deep Sea

Explore Your World: Weirdest Creatures in Time

Explore Your World: Creepiest Crawly Critters

EMMA FLANNERY   TIM FLANNERY

It's time to pop on your safari boots and walk among ...

EXTRAORDINARY ELEPHANTS

Hardie Grant
CHILDREN'S PUBLISHING

Illustrated by
KATIE MELROSE

MEET THE MAJESTIC ELEPHANT

Shhh! Do you spy a big animal with wrinkly grey skin and large floppy ears? Maybe you feel a trembling in the earth, then a deep rumble, and hear stumpy feet shuffling through the grass? Hold your breath – we're about to come face to face with a family of elephants.

The first thing you'll notice about an elephant is its size. They are the **largest land animals on Earth**, and can reach 3.2 metres, the same height as one adult human standing on top of another. They are also heavy, with the largest weighing about 11,000 kilograms – around the weight of 500 six-year-olds!

Elephants don't just have big bodies – they have **big brains** too. They're known for their long-term memory and their ability to learn and understand things.

Elephants are social creatures and COMMUNICATE with each other in many different ways: from loud calls to secret rumbles, and even through their pee!

3

Elephants can live to the ripe old age of 70. Unlike you or me, a male elephant continues to grow bigger throughout adulthood. Older males can be twice the size of younger males.

GET TO KNOW WHO'S WHO

You'll find elephants on only two continents: Africa and Asia. There are three species, or kinds, of elephant. Each species of elephant lives in its preferred natural home, or habitat, and so the three don't often bump into each other.

The **AFRICAN SAVANNAH ELEPHANT** is the largest kind of elephant and prefers to have more space to live in. The savannah is its habitat; it's a big grassy area with very few trees and elephants can often be spied munching on grasses and leaves.

The **AFRICAN FOREST ELEPHANT**'s habitat is the rainforest, where the trees are lush and close together and there is lots of yummy fruit to eat. They are the hardest to spot of the elephants, so scientists often look for their poo to keep track of them!

How can you tell if an elephant is from AFRICA OR ASIA?

You can look at the ...	AFRICA	ASIA
Size of its body	Bigger	Smaller
Shape of its head	Round	Two bumps
Size of its ears	Larger	Smaller
Tip of its trunk	Two finger-like tips	One tip

African elephant

Asian elephant

You can also tell the two kinds of African elephants apart if you look carefully enough. African forest elephants are slightly smaller and have rounder ears and straighter tusks.

The smaller **ASIAN ELEPHANT** lives halfway across the world from its African cousins, in Asia. It lives in both forest and grassy habitats. Around a third of all Asian elephants live in captivity – this means they are kept by humans, instead of living in the wild.

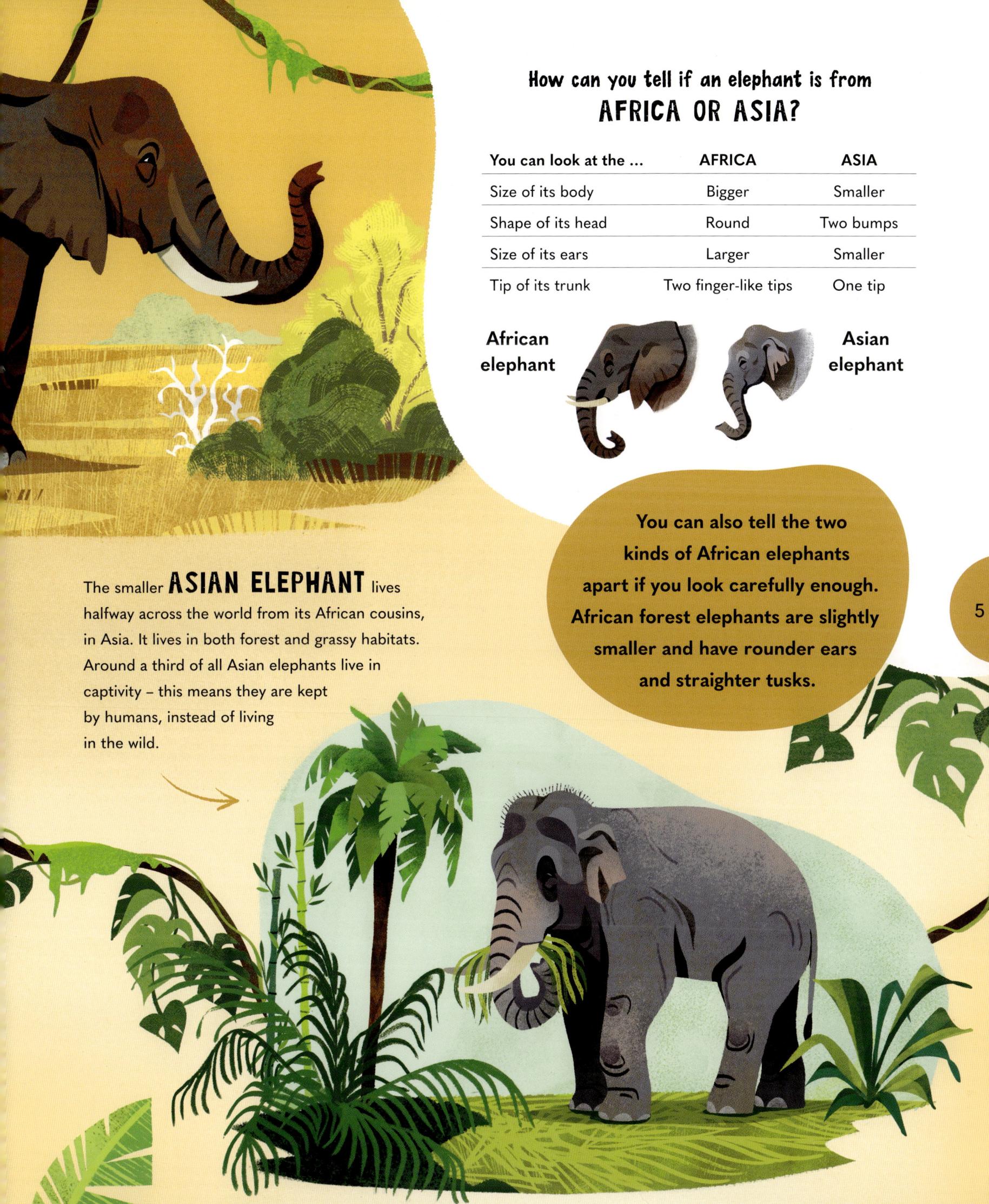

A CLOSER LOOK AT AN ELEPHANT'S BODY!

1

An elephant's body is covered in **thick, wrinkly grey skin**. If you touched an elephant's knees, the skin would feel rough and dry, like the bark of an old tree. But if you tickled an elephant under the armpit, the skin would feel soft! An elephant's skin is scattered with thick, tough hair, like the bristles on a broom. The wrinkles and hair on an elephant's skin help it stay cool in the heat of the sun.

2

Elephants have **tiny tails** that end in a tuft of hairs and are great for swatting away insects. Scientists identify individual elephants by looking at their tails, which are unique to each elephant.

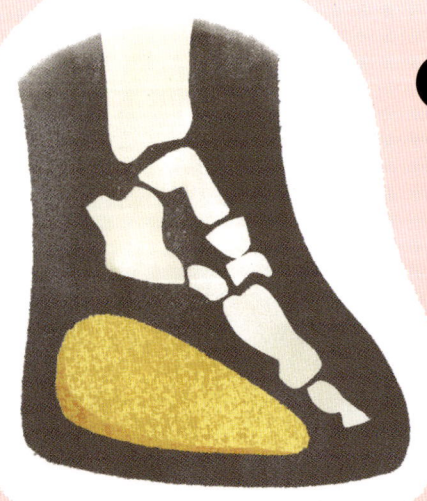

3

Elephants walk on their tiptoes! Their four hefty legs each end in a **stumpy foot** that looks flat because there is a large pad of fat behind their toes. Like you, elephants have five toes on each foot. But, unlike you, an elephant might not have a toenail on each of its toes!

4

Elephants have the **largest brains** of any land animal, which weigh up to 6.5 kilograms. This is about the same weight as a four-month-old baby!

5

An elephant doesn't sweat through its skin – it uses its big **floppy ears** to cool down by flapping them in the breeze, just like a fan.

6

Some elephants have **tusks,** which are long teeth that stick out from their mouths. Elephants use their tusks to dig, gather food, lift things and protect themselves. Tusks never stop growing, so the older and wiser the elephant, the longer its tusks are. Elephants can be left- or right-tusked, just like humans and their hands! The dominant tusk is usually slightly shorter because it is used more.

7

One of the funniest features of an elephant has to be its **trunk**, which is actually its nose and upper lip joined together. An elephant's trunk is strong, muscly and boneless – like our tongues. It is also one of the most sensitive body parts of any animal on the planet. Trunks do more than just smell – elephants use them to pick up objects, to eat and drink, to communicate with each other and even as a snorkel when they go swimming!

INTELLIGENT
CREATURES

Elephants have excellent memory.
Can you remember what you ate for breakfast last Tuesday? If you were an elephant, you might be able to! Elephants can remember smells, travel routes and the calls of other individual elephants for many years.

Some elephants recognize themselves in a mirror.
While this might not sound super smart, only a handful of animals can do this, including humans, apes and dolphins.

Elephants can use tools. They have been seen to pick off branches from a tree to swat pesky flies. In Bengaluru Zoo, India, an elephant was spotted picking up a twig with its trunk and using it to scratch an itch behind its ear!

Elephants dream. Elephants only dream once every three to four days, and only when they lie down to sleep. Most of the time elephants sleep standing up.

Elephants have a sense of humor.
When elephants play, they get creative and they have fun by finding things in their environment like sticks, plants and rocks to play with. Baby elephants have even been heard making a laughing sound during play. While baby elephants are the most playful, adults are known to have fun too!

Elephants have empathy, the ability to understand how someone else feels. Empathetic elephants form strong loving bonds with their friends and family and help or comfort others if they are in a pickle. For example, when an elephant is stuck in the mud another elephant will often come to help.

9

Elephants might even understand death and experience grief. When an elephant comes across the dead body of another elephant, it investigates the body for a long time in silence. Elephants have been seen to prod and poke the bones of dead elephants. Sometimes they even try to guard the body, or cover it with dirt. Mother elephants have been seen carrying the bodies of their dead babies with their tusks.

The trunk is a very handy body part for elephants – it can move in all directions and grip on to objects. Just like the tips of your fingers, an elephant's trunk can pluck a single blade of grass from the ground.

TRUNK-TASTIC!

Elephants use their trunks to collect food, whether it's from a tree or off the ground, and use the strong muscles of their trunks to smash it into a solid pile. When the elephant is ready to eat, it uses its trunk to move the clump of food into its mouth.

If an elephant can't reach its food with its trunk, it can use its body to get to the food. African forest elephants love eating *Omphalocarpum procerum* – a fruit that's twice the size of a tennis ball and found high up in the tree. To reach it, an elephant bumps its big body against the tree trunk to shake the fruit off the tree. It then uses its pointy tusks or strong jaws to crack the hard fruit open.

To drink, an elephant sucks water up its trunk and then squirts the water back into its mouth! An elephant's trunk has extreme suction and can suck up water at a speed of 540 kilometres per hour – that's 30 times as fast as your sneeze. Trunks can also act like a water balloon. An elephant can inflate its nostrils to hold a large amount of water – up to 45 litres! What a funny sight!

You might see an elephant using its trunk like a hose to cool down!

Elephants use their trunks to caress and smell family members, and to say hello to other elephants. When groups of elephants pass one another, they often stop to touch each other's trunks.

Because the trunk is such an amazing body part, scientists have studied how it works so they can build a robotic trunk. Imagine what you could do with your very own robotic trunk. It would be like having another hand so you could ride your bike and eat an ice-cream at the same time, or bake a cake while you tickle a friend's foot!

SMELL
LIKE AN ELEPHANT

Elephants have an incredible sense of smell. They often lift their trunks high up in the air, or move their trunk along the ground, to smell for food, water or pee from far away.

Elephant noses don't only smell food; they can even figure out how big or small the food is. If you hide two piles of seeds under separate buckets, an elephant's sense of smell will lead them to choose the bigger pile. The two piles can be really close in size, so close that even you wouldn't be able to tell which is bigger with your eyes. What an impressive nose!

12

Elephants might point their trunks in the direction of a smell that they've picked up. This gesture is called a PERISCOPE SNIFF!

Can you use your nose to smell water when it's hundreds of metres away or underground? I bet the answer is no. Well, an elephant can, and this talent would sure be handy on a hot day. Once its nose guides it close to water that's underground, it can use its tusks or feet to dig a hole to reach the water.

Why would an elephant want to smell stinky pee? An elephant can recognize which group member the pee belongs to, or tell if the pee was left by a male elephant searching for a mate. Imagine if you could recognize your family and friends just by the smell of their pee!

An elephant's nose can even sniff out a hidden bomb. Scientists set up an experiment to see if elephants could smell small amounts of hidden TNT, a kind of bomb. They smelled the bomb 99 per cent of the time.

EAT, POO, REPEAT!

Elephants have HUGE appetites. Being herbivores, they mainly have a plant-based diet, munching on plants, leaves, fruits and even roots. They spend up to 18 hours a day looking for food. The amount of food an elephant eats in a single day could keep you alive for a month or two.

Sometimes an elephant stays awake for a few days in a row so it can keep moving to find food or to stay away from danger. Elephants get around two hours of sleep every night, the shortest sleep time of any mammal. In comparison, adult humans sleep for around eight hours a night, but the younger you are, the more sleep you need. We'd be exhausted on an elephant's sleep schedule!

14

Elephants eat around 160 kilograms of food every day – the total weight of nine five-year-olds!

Elephants are most active at dawn and dusk – just before the sun rises and just after it sets.

Of course, all that food has to come out too, so an elephant poos around 10 times a day! Each poo weighs about the same as a border collie! You can tell a lot from elephant poo, including the size of an elephant's anus, or butt hole; once you know this, you can work out its age.

Luckily, elephant poo isn't stinky. Believe it or not, some people even think it smells nice! In some parts of the world, people light elephant poo on fire – the poo-scented smoke helps keep the mosquitos away.

Elephant poo is a great fertiliser and helps plants grow, but it can also move trees! When elephants eat fruit, they also eat the seeds inside. The seeds aren't digested and take around 40 hours to travel from an elephant's mouth to its butt. In that time, an elephant would've walked a great distance and when the elephant finally poos out the seeds, the seeds grow into trees in a location far away from the original trees.

WELCOME TO THE FAMILY!

Elephants live in herds, or groups, that are big and made up of many adult female elephants and their young. Who is in the herd can change over time. In tough times large elephant herds may split into smaller groups. When the groups reunite, the elephants greet each other excitedly, sometimes with a big roar!

In a herd, all females help to babysit the younger elephants. Babysitting is also a good way for teenage elephants to learn how to look after baby elephants.

African elephant families have a MATRIARCH, an older female who is the head of the family. Other animals that have matriarchs are meerkats, lions and killer whales.

A female elephant and her daughters share a strong bond – they will stick together for life.

When a male elephant becomes an adult, at about 14 years of age, he will leave his family and go on an adventure. Adult male elephants are always moving and searching for a mate. During their search, they sometimes spend time with other families or make friends with other adult males.

When a herd is on the move, the elephants might walk in a single line called a **procession**. Often the matriarch will be at the very back of the line, with a trusted female relative heading the procession.

TALK
LIKE AN ELEPHANT

Elephants make lots of noises to communicate, such as snorts, roars, trumpets and cries. Scientists have discovered more than 30 different types of elephant call.

Sometimes an elephant will give an excited **trumpet call** when a baby elephant is being birthed – yippeeee! When young elephants are playing, they can also give a nasal trumpet call, which sounds like a grown-up blowing their nose!

HONK!

Elephants also communicate with **deep rumbles**, which can travel up to 10 kilometres. Elephants feel rumbles with the tips of their trunks and the soles of their feet. Elephants can figure out who's talking by their rumble. Adult females can recognize 100 of their friends through their rumble alone.

Different kinds of rumbles can mean different things. A rumble for 'Let's go!' will be different to the one for 'I want to mate'.

19

Elephant rumbles are too low for human ears to pick up, but we can sometimes feel them if we try very hard.

American scientist Katy Payne was the first to discover that elephants talk through rumbles. She was at a zoo watching the elephants, to understand their behaviour, when she felt a vibration in the air. Next time you are at the zoo try hard to feel the elephant rumble.

GRAND GESTURES

Just as you might wave to a neighbour, elephants use gestures to communicate. An elephant can move parts of its body, like its ears, head, legs, trunk and tail, to send information to other elephants. How would you show these gestures with YOUR body?

20

I AM LISTENING TO A SOUND OR FEELING DISTANT VIBRATIONS

Freezing (not moving body)

Circus pose ('s' shape with trunk)

I AM WAITING

PLAY WITH ME!

Kneeling down

LOVE IS IN THE AIR

An elephant becomes ready to mate when it reaches around 14 years of age. Male elephants will leave their herd in search of a mate, and most female elephants usually have their first baby around this time.

When a male elephant is ready to mate, he enters a phase called **musth**. Musth lasts a few days for younger males and a few months for older males. During this time the male elephant becomes aggressive and energetic. He also has a sticky ooze coming out of the side of his head that makes him more aggressive, and smelly pee that drips down the back of his legs to let other elephants know he is searching for a mate.

GROSS!

A mother elephant takes a long time to raise her baby, and so she only has a few days every three to six years when she is ready to mate. This means there is great competition among males to mate with a female who is ready. Sometimes males will fight: they will ram one another with their heads, body and tusks.

When a female is ready to mate, she calls for a male, using a very powerful and deep rumble that can travel long distances. This rumble is so low that humans can't hear it. Male elephants search far and wide for a female to mate with, always listening out for a rumble to respond to.

Elephants can only mate with their own kind.

An elephant can use its trunk to be romantic – when elephants mate, they intertwine trunks.

HERE COMES THE BABY!

After elephants mate, a baby elephant grows in the female elephant's womb. A human baby grows in the womb for nine months before it is born. But elephant babies grow in the womb for 22 months – the longest time a mammal grows in a womb.

When an elephant is born, it can't rest for long – it gets on all four feet as quickly as possible. This is so it can move away from any danger. You will always find a baby elephant close to its mother because Mum means safety and survival.

Elephant mothers are the best teachers. They show their young how to do everything: how to find their way around, how to swim, what to eat and how to stay away from predators like lions and tigers.

Baby elephants and baby humans have a lot in common. Baby elephants like to suck their trunks just like baby humans suck their thumbs. Baby elephants lose their first set of teeth too! Baby elephants are also very playful – they like to play games like 'climb-upon', where they jump on top of one another and form a big wiggly pile. The baby elephants in the pile squirm and kick their legs out in glee!

It takes about a year for baby elephants to learn how to control their trunks. While they're learning, you might see them swinging their trunks in a very funny way! For the first few months, a baby elephant doesn't use its trunk to eat or drink. Instead, it is nursed by its mum, who provides nourishing milk for up to three years.

Elephants love their mums.

UNEXPECTED COUSINS

There is no animal on Earth that looks quite like an elephant, so its closest living relatives are sure to surprise you. Elephants have a bunch of weird-sounding creatures in their extended family. All of these animals share a common ancestor that lived around 60 million years ago in Africa.

How do we know these odd animals are related to elephants? Scientists look for similarities in body shape, teeth and bones, and also in DNA, the tiny genetic instructions found in all animals.

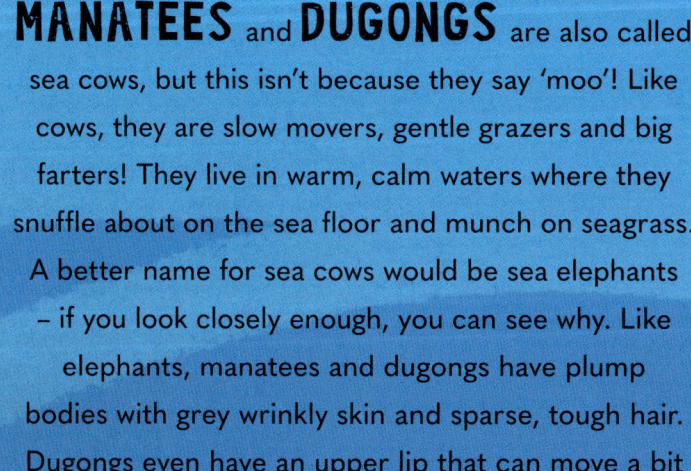

MANATEES and **DUGONGS** are also called sea cows, but this isn't because they say 'moo'! Like cows, they are slow movers, gentle grazers and big farters! They live in warm, calm waters where they snuffle about on the sea floor and munch on seagrass. A better name for sea cows would be sea elephants – if you look closely enough, you can see why. Like elephants, manatees and dugongs have plump bodies with grey wrinkly skin and sparse, tough hair. Dugongs even have an upper lip that can move a bit like a trunk, and some mature dugongs have tusks.

The **HYRAX**, also called a rock rabbit, is a small hairy creature that looks like a large guinea pig. But looks can be deceiving, because they are actually the closest living land relative of elephants! Hyraxes live in some parts of Africa and the Middle East and they weigh about the same as a small cat. If you zoom in on a hyrax's mouth, you can see two teeth at the front that stick out like tiny tusks. These keep on growing, just like the tusks on an elephant.

The **AARDVARK**, which means 'earth pig' in Afrikaans, lives in Africa in underground burrows. It has a pig-like snout, big bunny ears, strong claws for ripping open termite mounds, and a long sticky tongue to gobble its termite dinner up. Aardvarks and elephants are similar in a way that is hard to spot – the males have testicles that are hidden inside their body! Male hyraxes and sea cows also have hidden testicles.

Testicles produce sperm for reproduction and most male mammals have testicles on the outside of their bodies.

Its tusks were larger and curvier than an elephant's. It used its tusks to dig for food in the snow or to fight with other mammoths.

THE WOOLLY MAMMOTH

Elephants' closest relative was the woolly mammoth, but it became extinct 4,000 years ago. It lived during an ice age, when the world was much colder than it is today.

The woolly mammoth was about the same size as an African savannah elephant.

Woolly mammoth **African elephant**

The woolly mammoth had a hump on its back that was much like a camel's hump and it stored energy for when times were tough.

It had smaller ears than elephants, meaning less heat could escape from its body.

Just as its name suggests, the woolly mammoth was, well, woolly! Its warm, hairy coat helped it survive in its cold, icy home.

Even though mammoths became extinct thousands of years ago, you can still see the body of one today. After several woolly mammoths died, their bodies were preserved under the ice and snow for thousands of years until we found them. We call these mammoths 'mummified', as their skin and muscles can still be seen. There are even baby mammoth mummies that are on display in museums around the world.

Believe it or not, scientists are hard at work to bring the woolly mammoth back from the dead! They are using DNA extracted from frozen mammoth mummies and splicing it with the DNA of an elephant in the hope of making a baby mammoth.

The Asian elephant is more closely related to the woolly mammoth than it is to African elephants!

HOW INCREDIBLE!

THE FUTURE OF ELEPHANTS

All kinds of elephants are endangered, which means that they are at risk of becoming extinct and disappearing forever. When an animal goes extinct, it isn't just bad for them. Their extinction disrupts the food chain and balance of the ecosystem they belong to, and this can impact the wider environment and humans too.

Only 500 years ago there were more than 25 million elephants in Africa, but today there are just under half a million. Asian elephants have lost half of their population in the last 75 years. The African forest elephant is critically endangered, which is the last step before extinction.

Two main reasons why elephants are ENDANGERED:

Elephants have lost large areas of their habitats – for some, up to 90 per cent. Some forests where elephants live have been cut down by humans for wood, or to build farms, roads or buildings. The more space humans take, the less space elephants have to live in.

Some people illegally kill or poach elephants for their tusks. The elephants they kill are often the biggest, oldest and wisest elephants because they have the biggest tusks. Elephant tusks are called ivory, and ivory is used by people to make decorations or is ground down for traditional medicine.

NOW THAT YOU KNOW MORE ABOUT ELEPHANTS, DON'T FORGET TO SHARE WHAT YOU'VE LEARNED WITH EVERYONE YOU KNOW!

31

For Ginger and Nina

PROFESSOR TIM FLANNERY

is one of the world's leading scientists, explorers and conservationists. He has published more than 30 books, including the award-winning *Here on Earth* and best-selling *Explore Your World* books, many of which he co-wrote with his daughter Emma. He is a frequent presenter on ABC Radio, NPR and the BBC, and has also written and presented several series on the Documentary Channel.

EMMA FLANNERY

is a scientist and writer who has co-written many of the *Explore Your World* books with her father, Tim. Her curiosity for the natural world has seen her travel and work in some of its most wild and interesting places. Her passion for science has an infectious and playful enthusiasm that inspires curiosity in children and adults alike.

KATIE MELROSE

is an illustrator whose love for art and reading was cultivated at a young age by her parents. You'll mostly find her with a brush, but when she's without, she'll be in the kitchen, cooking up a storm and pretending she's a chef – perhaps her second greatest passion in life after illustration.

Hardie Grant acknowledges the Traditional Owners of the Country on which we work, the Wurundjeri People of the Kulin Nation and the Gadigal People of the Eora Nation, and recognises their continuing connection to the land, waters and culture. We pay our respects to their Elders past and present.

Hardie Grant Children's Publishing
Wurundjeri Country
Level 11, 36 Wellington Street
Collingwood Victoria 3066
Melbourne | Sydney | San Francisco
hardiegrant.com/childrens

ISBN: 9781761211713   First published 2024

A catalogue record for this book is available from the National Library of Australia

Publisher Marisa Pintado
Art Director Pooja Desai
Design Kelly Elphick
Editorial Joanna Wong with Emma Schwarcz
Production Amanda Shaw
Illustrator Katie Melrose
Printed and bound in HeShan China, March 2025
by LEO Paper Products LTD.

MIX
Paper | Supporting responsible forestry
FSC® C020056

The paper this book is printed on is from FSC®-certified forests and other sources. FSC® promotes environmentally responsible, socially beneficial and economically viable management of the world's forests.

2 4 5 3

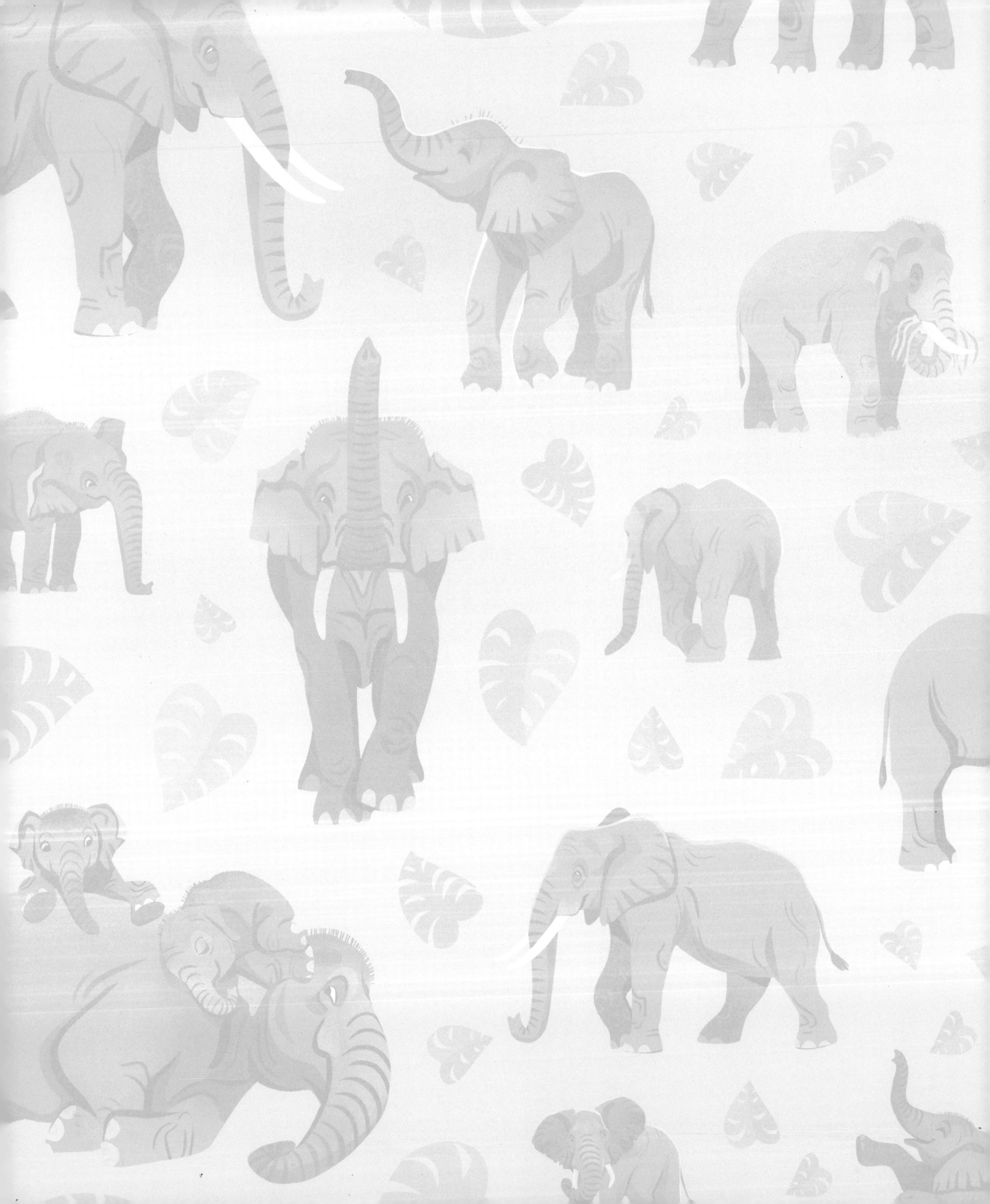